MAGICKAL SEX

Other titles by Fiona Horne

MAGICKAL SEX

A Witches' Guide to
Beds, Knobs and Broomsticks

Fiona Horne

Thorsons

Thorsons
An Imprint of HarperCollins*Publishers*
77–85 Fulham Palace Road, Hammersmith, London W6 8JB

The Thorsons website address is: www.thorsons.com

and *Thorsons*
are trademarks of HarperCollins*Publishers* Limited

First published by Thorsons 2002

1 3 5 7 9 10 8 6 4 2

© Fiona Horne 2002

Fiona Horne asserts the moral right to be
identified as the author of this work

A catalogue record for this book is available from the British Library

ISBN 0 00 714133 5

Motif by Dog-Eared Design

Printed and bound in Great Britain by
Martins the Printers Limited, Berwick-upon-Tweed

contents

Blessed Be

Louise McNamara, Karen Kreiger, Gary Shoefield,
Lesley Johnson, Joe Talbot and the UPC Broadcast crew,
Jo George, Hatty Madden, Megan Slyfield, Victoria
McCulloch, Dannii Minogue, Alan David, Miriam Kravitz,
Tom Hoberman, Yelba Quinn, Jodie Holdway,
Simone and Zoya at "dog-eared design" and ... You!

Please visit me at:
www.fionahorne.com

INTRODUCTION

**Everyone wants a magickal love and sex life.
This became profoundly clear to me as I hosted the
first series of my television show, *"Sexy Spells"*, in
the UK. I was flooded with letters and emails from
people needing enchanted advice and bewitching
solutions for all manner of love and sex problems,
which inspired me to write this book.**

You don't have to be a full-time Witch to be able to enjoy
the influence of magick in your life. You do, however,
have to have a few things in common with a full-time
Witch – that is, the ability to see nature as sacred, thus so
is the human body, human desire and our sexuality.

To work magick you need to suspend any disbelief and
fear and be prepared to accept that extraordinary things
can and do happen – the world is a magickal place!

In this book you will find ways to work with the power of
various herbs, crystals, colors, phases of the moon, and
Goddesses and Gods of different cultures to improve and
enhance your love and sex life. There are magickal
incantations to say and magickal tasks to do as well
as some practical, everyday advice to weave all your
efforts together and ensure success!

The most powerful tool you have to work with, though,
is your will – magick will work as well as you want it to
– so really concentrate and believe in your own
infinite abilities!

All the different herbs, crystals, colors and objects that
are used in the spells are aligned for their magickal
ability. These work like magnets to help ensure you

"attract" your goal – be aware of this and they will work for you. Also you will find as you explore this book that the same ingredients and objects are used repeatedly though in different ways – all effectively. So you don't have to go out and spend a lot of money and worry about trying to hunt down bizarre and rare items (though you can if you want to). However, I've picked everything for maximum magickal potency and accessibility.

Finally, the most important thing is to enjoy what you are doing. Witchcraft is just that – a craft – and the key to success is get creative and have fun!

Because remember:

"All acts of love and pleasure are sacred to the goddess"

baby bliss

SEXY SPELLS

My husband and I have a great sex life and a wonderful relationship. We have been trying to conceive a baby but with no luck. We've both been to the doctor and there is nothing wrong physically. Is there a spell we can do to help us get pregnant?

Well you can have a bit of fun with the following spell but it is based on ancient pagan fertility rituals that were taken very seriously in their day.

First you need to prepare a fertility oil by soaking a
handful of marsh mallow root in a cup of almond oil
overnight and straining into a glass bowl.
Place this by your bed.

Next prepare your bedroom for fertility magick by
sprinkling a mixture of salt and rice around the bed
(you can vacuum this up later!). Hang a bunch of
mistletoe above the bed or place it on the pillow – all
these are powerful fertility charms.

Light pale green candles and burn rose geranium essential oil in an oil burner to set a passionate and fertile mood.

Now you need to place a broomstick across the doorway. Not an old plastic one – a new one that has never been used for sweeping and has a wood handle and straw brush. The broom handle represents man, and this being inserted into the brush – which is woman – makes the broom a powerful symbol of procreation.

When the bedroom is ready, your husband and yourself should shower or bathe together. Make it romantic and sexy – you are bonding your bodies and spirits to unite in the wondrous creation of a baby. Use a natural shower/bath gel and wash each other to not only be clean but to remove any accumulated stress or worry. You both need to feel peaceful and confident.

Towel each other dry and walk naked to the bedroom.

As you enter you need to vocally reaffirm your desire to make a baby – look into each other's eyes and … jump over the broomstick! This mimics the customs of May Day or Beltane, the pagan spring fertility festival, and sends a message to the Universe that you want to conceive.

Before making love you and your husband should massage the fertility oil into each other's genitals – as you do this speak to each other of your love for each

other and your desire for a baby as the ultimate
expression of this love.

Make love slowly and passionately, all the time focusing
on and speaking of your desire for a baby.

You can do this fertility ritual more than once but
if you time it well (that is, whilst you're ovulating,
usually two weeks after the day your period started)
you really should conceive. Making babies is not
just about the union of bodies, it is about the union
of spirits – and this ritual works not only on the
physical plane but also on the spiritual.

yo-yo libido

SEXY SPELLS

My boyfriend and I have been together for two years and have always had great sex up until the last few months. He has trouble staying hard — he's up and down like a yo-yo! Have you got a spell to strengthen his libido?

There could be a number of reasons your boyfriend is having trouble and I would suggest a quick visit to the doctor's for a check-up. Sometimes stress and fatigue can cause problems – is he having a hard time at work? Are there money problems? If he's got all this under control, then I would suggest a two-fold approach to the problem – a few things for him to do and a few for you!

There are certain foods that are good for a man's libido and virility.

Stir some cinnamon into his morning coffee – just a quarter of a teaspoon. The added advantage is that it will

flavour his umm … sperm! True! Try it out – cinnamon
coffee in the morning and cinnamon … at night!

A food considered to enhance male virility is the humble
kidney bean. Because of its shape it is thought to represent the male testicles and is a powerful virility charm.
So whip up a yummy kidney bean casserole and hand
feed it to him wearing a sexy negligee! If your man
can't stand kidney beans (and not even the brilliant
recipe I have included here will tempt him!) there
are some other foods that will stir his juices :

Asparagus
Avocado
Garlic
Ginger
Shellfish such as shrimps, prawns, mussels, clams, scallops
and oysters
Eels
Steak
Fresh figs
Good quality chocolate

Kidney Bean Casserole
(SERVES 2)

1 tablespoon butter
½ onion, chopped
1 garlic clove, chopped
½ green (bell) pepper, chopped
1 teaspoon flour
1 teaspoon chilli powder
200g/1 cup canned chopped tomatoes
375g (13oz) cooked kidney beans, drained
Salt and freshly ground black pepper to taste
¼ teaspoon dried thyme
1 tablespoon chopped fresh parsley
2 tablespoons grated Cheddar cheese

Preheat the oven to 180°C (350°F) Gas mark 4.
Heat the butter in a frying pan or skillet and add the
onion, garlic and pepper. Cook until the onion has
softened, about 8 minutes. Add the flour and chilli
powder and stir thoroughly. Add the tomatoes, stir and
bring to a boil. Add the kidney beans, salt and pepper
to taste, thyme and parsley. Mix well and pour the
mixture into a medium casserole. Bake for 30 minutes.
Sprinkle with the cheese and bake for another 5 minutes.

Another potent symbolic food for men is the
chestnut – also known as "Jupiter's Nuts"!
Set up a "Virility Altar" featuring chestnuts in his

bedroom – or wherever you two make love. If you can't get chestnuts, any large round nuts will do!

On a bench or table-top place 2 red candles that you have rubbed some patchouli oil into (a powerful male aphrodisiac). In front of these place a bowl of chestnuts, a photo of your man and a piece of his … pubic hair!

So it doesn't blow away, pop the hair in a little amulet bag – purple or orange would be a good color. Have some sandalwood incense for personal empowerment. You can place some other phallic objects there as an offering to the God – bananas are good! Encourage your man to meditate a little at the altar every day, focusing on being confident and knowing that he is virile and potent.

Now you may find all this funny, but magick works with the intent you fuel it and all these objects work to trigger your man's subconscious into accepting that he is confident and virile again as well as sending a message to the Universe that he desires to be potent.

When you are making love, have the altar candles and the incense lit to power up the lusty vibes in the room. Now it's time for you to get to work exciting your man and making him feel relaxed and desirable.

Massage is a wonderful way to seduce, but give your skills more oomph by using a magickal massage oil featuring essential oils that will enhance his passion –

to one cup of almond or other plain massage oil, add six drops of patchouli and four of cypress. Have a bowl of the oil by the bed and dip both your hands into it, before sliding them over him. Make the massage slow and luxurious. Tease him with firm strokes followed by tickles and soft kisses all over his body.

If it's a bit "touch-and-go", just relax – don't comment on it whatever you do. Persevere and keep pampering him. Look at other areas that may be affecting his ability to perform and encourage him to address these problems as well.

However, I am confident that if you both focus you will have great results!

nervous
nineteen

SEXY SPELLS

I am 21 and my boyfriend is 19. I am his first lover
and he is very nervous. So far we have not been able
to have sex. Is there a "performance anxiety" spell
that will help him relax and get into it?

First and foremost, don't pressure him. You are also
young and you need to be compassionate and
understanding that he is not as sexually confident
as you. Believe me, you can sort this problem out quick-
smart as long as you don't scare him off! He's probably
nervous because he wants to please you and is scared
of doing something wrong.

To do some "performance magick" you will need to
get hold of two things – a herb called damiana and
some henna powder. You can get both of these from
a health food store.

Damiana is an aphrodisiac and henna is what the ancient
Egyptian, Arabian and Indian peoples used to color hair
and decorate the skin with. It is a dye that gradually
fades with time (usually a few weeks).

Mix a paste of the henna with water according to
directions. Take a small amount (about half a teaspoonful)
and mix into half a cup of olive oil. Put this aside
for use later. Make a brew of damiana tea – 3 teaspoons
of the herb to a pot. Strain and sweeten with plenty
of honey and then chill.

Now get creative. I suspect your attempts to make love
with your boyfriend have been in a bed with the pressure
on. You need to "ease" him into it and seduce him!
So I would suggest setting up a special area outside with
an open fire or perhaps in front of a fireplace
(not only beautiful, but the element of fire
encourages action and swift results!).

Adorn the area with cushions and soft rugs and incense
sticks sweetly scented with strawberry and musk. Fill
two goblets – or elegant glasses – with the damiana
potion and place the henna paint nearby.

Invite your boyfriend into this space and have him lie
down on the rugs in front of the fire. Give him a goblet

of damiana and tell him it's a herbal tea to relax him.
Don't give him a beer if he asks for one (that can
actually make things harder and I suspect you've already
tried breaking the ice with alcohol and it didn't work).

Tell him you want to honor him as a God, and ask if he
would let you worship him? Don't crack up laughing!
Concentrate and connect with the deep sense of
reverence that all humans should have for each
other – our sexuality is indeed a wondrous expression
of the life force and worthy of worship.

Give him some damiana potion to drink. It will taste
like sweet tea and encourage him to relax.

Now take a little of the henna oil and massage it onto
his penis. It will go a bit red! This is an ancient Arabic
tradition to encourage virility. (Wipe your hands with
a towel straight after or you will have red palms.)

Share the damiana together as a "loving cup". That is,
sip from the same cup and stroke his body lightly
to make him relaxed.

Now kiss him on his third eye (between his eyebrows)
and say:
"I honor and desire your mind"

Kiss him on his throat and say:
"I honor and desire your words"

Kiss him on his chest over his heart and say:
"I honor and desire your love"

And finally kiss him over his groin and say:
"I honor and desire your sex"

Gently stroke his penis and seduce him with kisses.
Most likely he'll be pretty turned on now – relaxed
and stimulated by the damiana potion and your
passionate attention!

Treat him like a God and he will act like one!

If you want to make the most of that Arabic tradition of
henna, do exactly as they did and massage a little into his
penis with the rising and the setting of the sun for seven
days to guarantee his potency!

looking for Mr Right

SEXY SPELLS

Every guy I seem to pick up is a dud — not only
in behavior but in bed! I guess I'm drawn to guys
that are tough and masculine, but they end up being
rough and insensitive. Is there some spell to help
attract the right partner?

Well you probably need to do some work on yourself,
examining your values and self-worth and working
out why you keep falling for the same kind of guy.
All brawn, no brain makes Jack a dull boy, so why
do you go for him?

So the first part of this magick is a self-awareness ritual
and the second a "come to me, man of my dreams" spell.

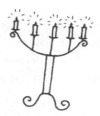

Sit naked in front of a mirror surrounded by a circle
of seven white candles for purity and spiritual
enlightenment. Burn sticks of sandalwood and
frankincense incense for wisdom and clarity. In each
hand hold a rose – a symbol of love and female sexuality.
Close your eyes and take a few deep breaths and take
your awareness inwards to a sense of inner peace.
Concentrate on what qualities you really desire in a man.
When you have a very clear vision and feel calm and
ready, open your eyes and gaze at yourself in the mirror.
Say:

"I am worthy of love, I am worthy of grace
passion and fulfilment take their place
in my heart and in my mind
the perfect man is now mine to find"

It's important that you have a really clear image
of the man you want in your life and also a strong
sense of self-worth. You deserve the best and you'll
settle for nothing less!

The next step of the spell is to conjure the man
of your dreams.

By the light of red candles, on a piece of red paper in
black pen write a description of the man you desire.
Don't specify the person – that would be interfering
with their free will and the spell would backfire.

Visualize the qualities you desire, perhaps:

Gentle caresses
Long sensuous kisses
Firm lovemaking
Laughs and good conversation
Friendship and fun

When your list is finished, pluck three petals from your roses and place on your list. Taking one of the candles, drip drops of wax on the petals to seal them and your desire to the paper, as you say:

"*Come to me*
man of my dreams
as is my will
So Mote it Be"

Fold the paper over so that the wax seals. Place this under your pillow. As you sleep you will have visions of your man – be on the lookout for him after this, because he will appear to you within 14 days.

Remember, magick works with the intent you fuel it with and with your desire – so suspend any disbelief and fear. The Universe is full of unimaginable potential and you can tap into this to realize your goals. Just believe in your own infinite potential and know that all the magick you need is inside you. You just have to unleash it.

leave the lights on!

SEXY SPELLS

*I love having sex and have been told I'm good in bed,
but I get really insecure if the lights are turned on.
I can only really loosen up in the dark. Is there a spell
to give me more confidence?*

To Witches, being naked is an utterly divine and pure
state – not just when you're a newborn baby, but all
through your life. Our bodies are miraculous and one of
nature's most profound expressions of the life force. One
of our greatest challenges in this modern age is to rise
above society's notions of what "looks good" and express
our own individual, unique and perfect beauty.

So the first thing I'm going to tell you to do is get naked.
In the privacy of your home start going starkers –

eat your breakfast in the nude, do the vacuuming, make the bed, whilst doing simple daily tasks get used to being naked. Now this might sound a bit silly, but it's actually very empowering. As much as you can, spend time outside without clothing too. Swim, sunbathe, even do some gardening – commune with nature as much as possible in your natural state and you will start to feel at ease and proud.

Now you can also mix up a magickal body love elixir to drink in the morning and a self love potion to massage into your skin morning and night to affirm your unique beauty.

To make the elixir, pour a pint of almost boiled spring water into a bowl and float two handfuls of fresh scented rose petals in it. Cover with a cloth and allow to steep

overnight. In the morning strain and mix in
1 tablespoon of brandy and four teaspoons of sugar.

Keep in the fridge and drink half a cup morning and
night. The rose is a sacred flower of love and beauty –
as you sip your elixir ask for the blessings of Aphrodite,
the Goddess of Love:

"Bless me lovely Aphrodite
As today I honor my special beauty"

TO MAKE A BODY LOVE POTION

Take a handful of scented rose petals and a handful
of marigold petals. Place these in a pan and pour over
a cup of almost-boiling water, cover with a cloth for a few
hours and then strain. To each 4 ounces of unscented
moisturizer cream (not lotion – Sorbolene is good) mix
in a ¼ cup of the flower infusion, whisking so that it
doesn't go too runny. You can also add 1 or 2 teaspoons
of very finely ground orris root powder (a powerful love
and romance attractor) to thicken if necessary.

Now add 5 drops of rose geranium essential oil
and mix through.

Store the body love potion in the fridge and, after giving
it a good shake, massage the cool, divinely-scented cream
into your body morning and night, and as you do so
concentrate on feeling proud of your body and blessed
by your unique beauty. The potion will be good for your
skin, the massage good for your spirits and the flower
essences good for your heart.

Also next time you're making love with the light on, try easing into it with the wonders of candlelight! Lots of red and pink candles will encourage passion, burn some ylang-ylang essential oil for sensuality and confidence and you will be free and willing!

afterplay delights

SEXY SPELLS

My boyfriend is a good lover and we get along great, but as soon as we have finished having sex he just rolls over and goes to sleep! I like cuddles and talking after sex but he just snores. Is there a spell I can do to make him more affectionate after we make love?

I've got a fairly simple suggestion straight up, that doesn't really have to do with magick – just a bit of psychology. Stop having sex in bed! If you have sex in a location where he can't just roll over and go to sleep it will help encourage him to break this annoying habit.

Why not seduce him outside on the patio after lunch? Or during a nice dip in the pool? What about over the kitchen table after breakfast? It's likely these unorthodox methods will spice up your sex life a bit and have the added advantage of taking it out of the "routine". That is, he won't feel like nodding off after having sex.

The only thing you can't do is have sex in bed for a while until he gets used to giving you some attention before and after! There is also some magick you can make to encourage his attention and make him more sensitive to your needs …

Burn some sandalwood incense to create a sacred space. Then take two white candles – carve your name in one and his name in another. Anoint them both with a little olive oil and then roll them in cinnamon – the olive oil is to bond them and the cinnamon is for increasing passion. Stand them next to each other – very close.

Close your eyes and meditate for a moment on your
desired outcome – remember, spells work with the intent
you fuel them so focus hard and when you have a very
clear vision of the two of you after making love hugging
and talking, light the candles and say this invocation:

*"Fire speed my wish to me
as is my will, So Mote it Be"*

Let the candles burn and as they do they should melt
together, fusing the two of you together in the
vision you have.

You won't be able to get him to leave you alone!

In Witchcraft we generally don't cast spells that can
interfere with another's free will – hence be aware
that you might want to fall asleep after sex one night
and he will be annoying the hell out of you with his
chatter and prodding!

bored out
of my brain

SEXY SPELLS

I am bored with my sex life. My partner is sweet,
but he just doesn't do it for me any more. I don't really
want to have an affair but I feel like I've hit a dead end.
Is there any way to spice up my sex life?

Well first I must say: "the world answers according to the
questions you ask it" and if you have got it into your head
that sex with your partner is boring then it will be! There
are plenty of things to do to spice up your sex life,
magickally and practically. First I think, though, you need
to affirm your love and connection to this person. Now,
you say you don't want to have an affair, but I do think
you need to do some work to really honor your love.

Invoking the energies of Aphrodite, the Goddess of Love,
will reinvigorate your passion.

Take two big, green apples (sacred to Aphrodite),
cut the cores out, keeping the seeds, and stand them
upright. Now take two gold candles and carve your
name in one and your lover's in the other. Anoint the
candles with rose oil to bless them, and stand them in the
apples. Make an altar in your bedroom with the apple
candles, sprinkling a circle of rose petals around them
both and burning rose and sandalwood incense.
Every Friday (sacred to the Goddess of Love) scatter
more rose petals and light the candles and know that
your love is being ignited. Meditate on the candle
flames and see visions of you and your lover in a
passionate embrace, with all your emotional and sexual
needs being utterly fulfilled. You can continue this
spell indefinitely but you will need to replace the
apples every couple of weeks! Just bury the old ones.

Your will is the greatest asset you have to working magick; if you start to imagine a different reality it will manifest. So now that you've got your spell-casting, brewing, metaphysical results you can do some work on the physical plane.

Now have you considered a bit of "role playing" to juice things up a bit? What if your lover was to come home one night from work and find a lusty medieval wench or an exotic Moulin Rouge dancer waiting for him?

Have a feast prepared for him with wine and sumptuous foods. Have the house lit with candles and scented with pungent, sexy incense, like patchouli and amber. Have fancy garments laid out for him and slowly undress him

from his normal persona and then clothe him in his new
one. Make sure you stay in character! You are performing
an enchantment here and taking your everyday life out of
the mundane into the realm of the extraordinary!

Then see where the evening takes you! The next
morning give him a token of your love and passion –
remember the seeds from your love apples? Well put
half each in two little red pouches – give him one
pouch to keep in his pocket and tell him to think of
you and your night of passion whenever he touches it.
Keep the other pouch close to you and you will
both maintain a lusty, loving bond and your sex life
will just get hotter and hotter!

desire me

SEXY SPELLS

There is a guy at work I really like — in fact I would love to seduce him! Is there a spell I can do to make him fall for me?

You're heading into dangerous waters here. To cast a spell over someone else for selfish purposes is to break one of the three main Witch Laws – *"Do what you will, but don't interfere with another's free will."* So if you attempt to make this guy fall for you, be prepared for nasty repercussions. He may well fall for you but you might find you're better off without his interest. Someone I know did a "Come to Me" spell and it worked very well – though unfortunately the guy turned out to be a bit of a psycho and she ended up very unhappy. It is far better to do a general "Come to Me" spell. Instead of specifying a specific person, you ask for a person with your chosen qualities and attributes – and let the Universe decide who is best for you. Having warned you, and you're thinking: *"Blow it! I like trouble, give me the spell!",* here it is.

You need to get hold of something that has his energy.
Some soil scooped from a footprint he has made,
or perhaps some body bits – hair, fingernails
(the girl I knew who did this spell offered him
a manicure at work – creepy!) or even spit
(a glass from which he has taken a sip).

Prepare for the spell by taking a bath to which you
have added half a cup of bath salts and 5 drops of lemon
oil (or a ½ cup of the juice). Lemon and salt work to
purify you and protect you from negativity. As you lie
in the bath focus on your intent, picture the guy in
your head and say the mantra:

"Come to me, come to me" over and over.

Do this spell in an enclosed private place. It is a work
in progress and must not be disturbed.

Sprinkle a circle of salt within which you will work, and
assemble a large red candle, white cord and "come to
me potent paste". Make this by mixing half a cup of
water with cornflour until it thickens. Add a teaspoon
of damiana (for passion), a teaspoon of cinnamon
(for potency) and 6 black peppercorns (for speedy
results). Mix this through and then add some of your
own saliva – or, for really potent results, masturbate
and add some of your vaginal fluid.

Carve his name into the candle and then place it in the
centre of a large plate and sprinkle the body bits or soil
around it. Take some of the paste and smear it over the

carving of his name, have a clear vision of his face in
your mind as you say:

*"Come to me my will is great
now you can't escape your fate"*

Take the white cord and trail it across your body,
visualizing it absorbing your energy, your lust, your
desire. Then wrap it around the base of the candle
as you say:

*"Bound to me, you now be
as is my will, So Mote it Be"*

Light the candle flame and gaze at the flame
as you intone:

"Come to me, come to me"

When you have a clear vision of the two of you
together, snuff the flame and say:

"It is done"

Cover the candle and plate with black cloth and leave.
Every night for the next seven days, smear more paste
on the candle, relight and again chant *"Come to me"*
– he will be yours within the week.

This is quite a sinister spell – I am assuming your motives
are harmless fun – but as I said earlier, interfering with
another's free will is breaking the laws of Witchcraft and
you will have to accept repercussions – threefold (at
least!). So think hard before you try using magick to
seduce another – and perhaps do a self-love spell to
enhance your natural charms and then when he falls
for you, you will know that it is really you that he
desires and not trickery and enchantment.

on the prowl

SEXY SPELLS

I am single and I love meeting women and having one-
night stands — not very politically correct I know.
My problem is that as much as I love doing this I
don't get much action! I'm not bad-looking, but is
there a spell that would improve my chances?

Well at least you're honest. I do have a spell for you and
it has an added advantage – it promotes safe sex, something you need to be very conscious of if you're running
around and hopping into bed with all and sundry!

This spell will help you to magickally charge your
condoms and guarantee their usage!

Before you head out for the evening, light a purple
candle for success and burn musk incense for lust.
Get dressed with intent, consciously focusing on your
goals for the evening as you adorn yourself.

Now pick out your favorite condoms, as many as you
think you can use and in your power color – maybe red
for passion, black for mystery, blue for happiness, green
for fun, natural for pride – whatever resonates
strongest for you.

Hold the condoms in your hand and focus on your goal.
In your mind's eye see yourself meeting interesting,
sexy people and having your pick of the bunch! See
yourself in bed with the woman you want, taking out
your power condom and making good use of it!

When the vision is very clear, open your eyes,
gaze at the candle flame and say:

"Power of fire, heed my desire.
My vision is clear — fuelled by desire.
On this night, without delay.
Passionate sex will come my way."

Snuff the candle flame and say, "So Mote it Be."

Pocket your condoms, head out and I expect you to use
every single one of them! Also seeing as you are using
magick to increase your chances of achieving your
desires, you owe the Universe something back. Why not
offer it "honest intent" – that is, be very clear with your
"conquests" and "partners" about your intentions. Don't
mislead a girl into thinking your objective is more than a
bit of overnight fun. Be honest with your intent and your
magick will work better and no one will get hurt.

sacred sex

SEXY SPELLS

I want to draw everyone's attention to the wonderful
practice of sacred sex.

Sex can not only be fun, hot and horny, it can also be
profound. A sacred sex ritual can have you tapping into
the divine joy that is found at the core of all creation.
It is all about how you approach it and, like all magick,
the intent with which you fuel your actions.

The following sex ritual honors and illuminates your
inner Goddess and God as well as spreading loving
energies into the Universe.

Another bonus of this ritual is if you and your lover
have a shared wish – perhaps you want to buy a house
together, or maybe have a child, or even have the money

to go on a holiday. You can use the sacred energy of
your combined orgasms to manifest your goal!

Prepare the space for your ritual by making an altar.
Burn ylang-ylang and coconut incense to represent
air and passion; burn red and pink candles for fire and
lust; clear and rose quartz crystal for earth, love and
manifestation; and a bowl of water with a flower floating
in it (something opulent like a tiger lily) for water
and emotional fulfilment. Also have two goblets of
wine ready to toast your efforts with later.

In front of the altar spread cushions and rugs
for sensuous comfort.

Your partner and you should bathe separately, focusing
on the ritual at hand. When you are both ready stand

nude in front of the altar facing each other, and to
commence the ritual the woman stamps the ground
three times and says:

"Man, you are potent and drive me wild with desire"

Then the man stamps the ground three times and says:

"Woman, you are lovely — join with me for I am afire"

(or both create your own words that express your
honor and desire for each other).

Then the woman dips her finger in the water and traces
the Witches, magick star over the man – the center of the
forehead, right nipple, left shoulder, right shoulder,
left nipple and back to the center of the forehead,
saying as she finishes:

"Thou art Blessed"

The man then dips his finger and does the same for
the woman, saying:

"Thou art Blessed"

Now you both should slowly start to stroke each other
to awaken each to subtle pleasures and ultimately great
passion – focusing all the while that you are in a
sacred space and that this is a ritual that celebrates
and honors all Creation.

When you are making love it is time to start focusing on
your desired goal if you have chosen to have one. Stare
into each other's eyes and let your passion build within.

As you both reach your peak, concentrate hard and come
together visualizing your goal and sending out your
request to the Universe on the wings of your desire.

After your union, drink the wine together and save a
little from each cup to pour on the ground as a libation
to the Goddess and God after the ritual.

You can keep your sacred sex altar set up as a reminder
of your love and the sacred nature of your union.
Also this is a wonderful ritual to do on the full moon
– a perfect time to do spell-casting of all sorts, but
particularly love and sex magick.

party time – it's Beltane!

SEXY SPELLS

I'm going to tell you all about one of the Witches' Sabbats. Sabbats are holy days or festivals and there are 8 each year. The one I'm going to describe now is called Beltane and it is a fertility festival – one of the most sacred times of the year.

The pagan holiday of Beltane (1, May northern hemisphere/ 31 Oct southern hemisphere) marks the beginning of summer. Beltane is a celebration of the new life that has emerged from barren winter, and for modern pagans represents the life-giving union of their Lord and Lady. Many May Day customs have their source in the Beltane rituals of pagan Britain, most of which were suppressed by the Church as it struggled to gain supremacy over the existing pagan religions of the British

Isles. One of the best-known folk customs associated with Beltane involves having sex out in the fields to ensure that the next year's crop will be bountiful.

There was also something called "the Sacred Marriage" enacted during these festivals of old. A man and woman, crowned King and Queen of the land, would publicly copulate to guarantee fertile land and an abundant harvest.

Witches celebrating Beltane now don't go around having sex in public – they would be arrested! But there are plenty of fun, potent, modern ways to honor this great time.

Invite some friends over explaining to them that you are having a party to celebrate all the good and abundant things in life. Ask them to each bring a bowl of seasonal food – that is, fruits and vegetables that are ripe at the time. Beltane festivals were traditionally fire festivals so, if you can, hold your gathering outside with fire stoked with wood and dried lavender – otherwise, a fireplace or lots of red, pink and purple candles will convey the life-changing passion of fire.

Decorate your space with lots and lots of flowers, so there is an overwhelming sense of abundance and beauty. Have plenty of wine (a light red would be good) and, if you like, mead and other hearty drinks. Sticks of rose and jasmine incense can sweetly scent the air and inspire in all gathered a relaxed and sensuous mood.

As a part of your Beltane ritual share wine, food and stories about all the good things in life. Celebrate

your successes and triumphs and talk about
your plans for the coming year.

After dinner it's time to honor the Gods. Ask everyone to
gather in a circle and hold hands as you say:

"Blessed be the Goddess of Life Eternal
Blessed be the God of the Powers of Life
Gathered tonight we celebrate our existence
And in each other's arms we taste our sustenance"

Now it's time to make love – if you're all comfortable you
can just get down to it! Otherwise, maybe separate into
different rooms. On this night more than any other it is
appropriate to experiment with the charms of another, so
if everyone is consenting feel free to bond with another's

lover – all the time knowing that this is a sacred
celebration of the forces of life.

Beltane is a wonderful festival – truly liberating and
honest. Our sexuality is one of the most profoundly
divine gifts that we can enjoy – in modern times much
exploited. But the ancient practices of this festival
can liberate you into having a truly healthy
appreciation of your sacred sexuality.

tantric temptation

SEXY SPELLS

Some men and women have asked me about achieving multiple orgasms magickally. Women have the pleasure of being multi-orgasmic by design – it's not so easy for a guy. But with practice and focus men can achieve the ability to orgasm more than once in a lovemaking session. The secrets are to be found in the practices of tantric sex. Whilst not being the exclusive domain of Witches – it is actually Eastern in origin – it is a practice that is aligned to a Witch's affinity with personal empowerment and joy.

Tantric loving can help with stress relief as it harmonizes and balances the energies of life. When a couple engage in tantric sex they develop a profound appreciation of each other as well as an enhanced sex life.

Tantra is a complex and evolved philosophy that can't
be taught in a few minutes. However, I can give you
some insights that you can try straight away.

Tantric loving is a lot more than genital stimulation.
Sit opposite your partner and gaze into their eyes –
together reach out and gently stroke each other and as
you do this attempt to harmonize your breathing. Focus
on allowing your Heart chakra – the energy centre of
your body in the centre of your chest – to glow with pure,
pale green light. See that light extend from your body
and connect with the Heart chakra of your partner.
Together be aware of this connection.

Both of you no doubt will be turned on now – it's important to remember that tantric sex is not so much about multiple orgasms as it is about prolonging the divinely pleasurable sensation of orgasm for as long as possible.

A good position to experiment with tantric sex is for the man to sit upright and for the woman to straddle his lap. This way she can control the proceedings!

Slowly start to make love – and any time either of you feel like coming, ease off and slowly start again. A good way of stopping the urge for a man to come is to squeeze his penis just below the head. Stretch out your lovemaking for as long as you can and be aware of the way the

sensations in your body start to change and evolve.
Continue to focus on breathing together and connecting
with each other's Heart chakra.

When you finally do decide to orgasm be conscious of
the movement of energy up from your genitals. Visualize
your orgasm as a stream of pure white light shooting up
through your body, through your Crown chakra (the top
of your head) and offer it out into the Universe as a
divine expression of your appreciation of being alive.

Tantric lovers balance their energies – including moods,
drives and desires. This results in an open, balanced relationship that continues to grow, fuelled by love and
divine passion in such a profound way that they truly
become like Gods. The fact that they become experts
in the sack is just a lovely bonus!

honor your Goddess

SEXY SPELLS

This is for the boys (and of course some girls!).
An Aphrodite ritual is something really special and
magickal that you can do for your female partner.

So I am going to show you how to spoil and honor
your partner in a way that will truly make her feel
like a Goddess.

The Greek Goddess of Love, Aphrodite, to be exact.
Honoring the presence of this Goddess in your lover will
awaken her to her true beautiful and deepest
sensuality – something you will benefit from too!

The legend of Aphrodite says she was born from the
ocean carried aloft on a scallop shell – so this ritual
will take place in the bathroom. Transform your

bathroom into an ocean paradise. Place shells of different sorts and beautiful pink and white flowers around the bath, illuminate the bathroom with the glow of pink candles – into each carve a heart and your initials, representing your love for your partner. Burn essential oils of rose geranium and orange flower.

Pink is Aphrodite's sacred color and you can make beautiful magickal bath salts very easily to turn the bath into a perfect pink pool of love.

In a large bowl mix:
1 cup of Epsom salts
¾ cup of baking soda
⅓ cup table salt

Mix these through and then add 6 drops of orange
flower oil, 2 drops of lavender, 2 drops of ginger, stir it
all through with a spoon and then slowly add drops
of pink food coloring – stirring through until the
salts are tinted pink.

Run the bath very warm – but not too hot – and pour
the salts in stirring them to dissolve. Then float a few
handfuls of fresh rose petals on the surface of the bath.
Put some beautiful, sensual music on, preferably
instrumental as lyrics can be distracting.

You have now created an environment fit for a Goddess.

Welcome your lover into the sacred space you have
created – gently disrobe her and help her into the bath.

Using a soft cloth, sponge her down, slowly and
seductively. Give her a glass of sweet champagne to
sip as she enjoys your attentions.

Read her some poetry that expresses your
deep feelings for her:

"Lady of the threefold shifting light,
Whose form is Earth, by day and night,
And yet about you flows eternal ocean,
Goddess so still, yet in perpetual motion.
Moon, sister-self and triple aspect of the Triple One,
Maiden, God creator, wise and ancient Crone.
Thou who art Earth, and Moon, and Sea,
Mother of All, thou madest me.

From your dark bones, from green and flesh,
From crystal waters and the quiet wind's breath,
These came from you, and now are me,
Eternal spirit clothed in frailty.
Yet beyond these there endless dwells
A light that from some star-seed fell.
Goddess of Life and Love and Paradox,
Keeper of the keys to all the locks,
Of Mysteries, of Earth and Sky,
Pray answer me. Who am I?"

Ask if you may join her in the bath and if she agrees
(I'm sure she will) then make love to her reverentially.

The energies of unconditional love that you have
conjured will consume both of you in holy passion.

As you pleasure her say:

*"You are a Goddess, blessed by the stars
it is the greatest honor to hold you in my arms"*

You need to make some effort, but anything worthwhile
needs effort and I promise you, spoiling your partner like
this will give you more brownie points than even if you
took her to the Ritz for the weekend!

Aphrodite is a generous Goddess and when she is
honored in this way the benefits will permeate every area
of your life for days after the ritual – people will treat you
kindly and express unexpected generosity –
and your love life will be incredible!

honor your God

SEXY SPELLS

Ladies (and men if that's your choice!) I'm going to show
you how to honor and awaken your man to the lusty
energies of Pan, Lord of the Forests.

Pan is the half man/half beast pagan God of Fertility.
His domain is lust and sex and fun so I'm sure that
you will enjoy this ritual as much as your man!

Choose a place in your garden that is as wild and foresty
as possible (but not too overgrown – you want to be
comfortable!). Otherwise, decorate your bedroom with
lots of green growing branches, pine cones and other
natural objects. Make a blend of essential oils as an
offering to your man.

Into ½ a small bottle of jojoba or almond oil add, 3 drops
of patchouli, 2 drops of juniper, 1 drop of pine and 1
drop of cedarwood. This is Pan Oil and your man can
wear this any time he wants to invoke the God in himself.

Light your space with green and orange candles each
carved with a heart and your initials to express your
adoration and desire for him.

If you can, light a fire and place some soft rugs in front
of it. Have some glasses of rich malted beer or a hearty
red wine ready and welcome your man into the sacred
space you have created.

Offer him the drink and tell him that you want to
worship him as a God. The best way to honor Pan is
to dance and play, be cheeky and seductive. Tickle your

man with feathers, cover him with kisses, massage richly scented oils into his skin. Anoint him at his throat and groin with the special blend you made for him and offer the rest as a gift.

Read him some poetry to honor his Godliness:

"Thrill with lissom lust of the night,
O man, my man!
Come careening out of the night
Oh Pan oh Pan
Come over the sea from Sicily and Arcady!
Roaming as Bacchus, with fauns and bards
And nymphs and satyrs for thy guards
On milk-white ass, come over the sea
To me to me! To me to me!"

(Aleister Crowley)

Put some music on and dance seductively for him. And when he's ready let him ravish you like a beast!

Pan is a happy God – and expressing wanton abandon is to honor him in a sacred way! So get as crazy as you like – laugh and make this ritual a time that your partner and you will never forget! Expect the spirit of Pan to reign in your man for some time to come – every time he anoints himself with the magickally charged oil you gave him he will feel those lusty feelings stir and won't be able to keep his hands off you!

all by myself

SEXY SPELLS

I don't have a boyfriend or partner, but I'm interested
in doing sex magick. Is there anything I can do?

Absolutely! Solo sex magick involves masturbating to
orgasm to raise power. As a woman you can focus on
the awesome power that you have to create, carry
and nurture life within you, and channel this to fuel
your desire. If you're a guy trying out this spell, don't
just think about Playboy, think also about your
body's incredible ability to create life.

It's very simple and only requires concentration
and purity of intent:

First bathe yourself with the intent to remove any
accumulated stress and impurities of emotion.

The reason you are focusing on this is because most people are brought up to feel uncomfortable with their sexuality and you want to bypass any inhibitions and allow yourself to connect with the divine, empowering gift of orgasm.

After you have bathed, burn some incense, perhaps sensual ones like ylang-ylang and patchouli or a more spiritual choice like frankincense or sandalwood.

Sit naked in front of a lit, white candle and meditate on the aim of your spell. It may be that you want a new boyfriend, or a new job, or a new direction in life. You need to get a very clear vision of what you desire in your head.

When you are ready start to stroke your body to awaken
it to subtle energies – keep concentrating on your goal.
When you are ready start to masturbate, again
concentrating on your goal and at the same time
allowing your passion that is building to express
your desire for your goal.

Feel the urge to orgasm build inside you, but delay it
for as long as you can – having to think about your goal
can help here! The longer you hold off, the more
power will be generated.

When you feel the ultimate peak approaching, focus as
hard as you can on your goal and then release the
orgasmic energy. See it rise up like lightning through
your body, shooting out of the top of your head and
into the cosmos to fuel the manifestation of your wish.

After your orgasm take a deep breath and say out aloud:

"It is done"

And it's as simple as that! Actually solo orgasm magick sounds a lot easier than it is – but once you master self-control and learn to channel the incredible energy that is raised during orgasm, it can become a very potent fuel for transformation.

Witchy foreplay

SEXY SPELLS

*You've talked about doing magick after sex —
what about foreplay? Is there a way of making
that magickal too?*

Well, I guess when you get foreplay right it's pretty
magickal anyway but there are Witchy ways of charging
it up and making it really potent.

The four elements of earth, air, fire and water are the
natural tools of transformation that a Witch works with.
You can incorporate these into your foreplay to really
prepare for the magickal act of making love.

The first element is earth
The best way to connect with earth energy is to make
love outside! Set up a beautiful, comfortable
environment under the stars or sun in which to
play. If this isn't possible you can capture the energy
of earth inside with crystals, like clear and rose quartz,

placed around the area you are getting passionate within! Be aware of the grounding nature of earth – the reassurance and comfort that it provides.

The next element is fire

Burn candles to illuminate your lovemaking and why not get a little more interactive and work with the exciting heat of fire – drip wax over your partner to surprise and seduce them – being aware of the power of fire to regenerate and purify.

The next element is air

Air can be connected with by burning incense and using … feathers! Tickle your partner with soft feathers, brush

them seductively over each other's skin and be aware
of air's ability to transform and carry on its breath new
beginnings and change.

And finally the element of water

Water represents emotion and connection – play with the
element of water by using its manifestation as ice. Watch
ice melt into water as you trail it over your partner's body
and be aware that water not only forms 70 per cent of
our planet's presence, but 70 per cent of our own bodies'.

The four elements can be played with – but making
magick is always about the intent you fuel your actions
with and if you incorporate the above practices with
a focused attitude, you will not only delight your
physical senses, but your spirit's too.

magickal massage

SEXY SPELLS

It's always wonderful to give and receive the sensual,
physical pleasure of massage – but you can also
stimulate the spirit when you rub your lover and
really give an incredible experience.

There are seven major energy centers of the body, called
"chakras", and when you focus you can stimulate these
and, during massage, not only relax muscles, but align
head, heart and soul.

Create a relaxing atmosphere with candles and incense
of sandalwood and myrrh. Lay your lover down on their
stomach, and ask them to breathe deeply.

Breathe deeply yourself and attempt to harmonize
your breathing with theirs.

Start to massage, in slow, firm circles, the base of their spine – this is the first chakra – the Root chakra. See it as a kind of "wheel" in an earthy, deep red color – and feel it pulse. When that vision is clear, sense the wheel starting to spin in a sunwise (deosil/clockwise) direction. Feel the strong centring action of this first chakra as it spins. Now, see it extend as a beam of red light deep, deep down into the earth, grounding and connecting the core of your partner with Gaia, the Earth Mother.

When you sense that connection to be really strong, ask your lover to turn over and move your attention to the next chakra: the Base Sexual chakra, which is just above the pubic bone. Gently circle your hands in a sunwise direction and see the chakra as a clear yet intense orange, like a huge eruption from a volcano, bubbling and pulsing.

Move to the next chakra, the Solar plexus, located at the base of the ribcage (the home of "gut" feelings). Gently circle your hands as you see it spin and pulse, its color pure yellow like marigolds.

Now to the Heart chakra. Massage a little firmer now and see it spin and pulse a soft green, the color of delicate new blades of feathery grass.

Move up to the Throat chakra. With your thumbs gently massage and see it spin and pulse the azure blue color of a fresh, clear daytime sky.

Next is the Brow chakra, or "third eye"; again with your thumbs massage in a circular motion and see it spin and pulse a rich, dark blue – the color of a deep tropical ocean.

Finally, move your attention to the Crown chakra, sitting behind your lover's head and giving them a lovely scalp massage – see the chakra manifest at their crown as a crystal-clear light purple, like a violet sky at sunrise. Concentrate on it spinning and pulsing, and channel this to the Universe. See a bolt of infinite diamond-white light come from the heavens and connect with your lover's Crown chakra.

As you visualize this see the light charge through your lover's glowing chakras, intensifying their colors and making them spin faster and faster. Then, see the white light shoot through the red cord of your lover's Root chakra descending into the earth and concentrate on grounding them with the purest of energy. See your lover's chakras glowing like a string of beautiful colored pearls.

When you are ready release any excess energy by placing your hands on the ground and letting it flow into the earth. Give your lover a cuddle and perhaps make love, sharing in the sacred energy that you have just conjured.

Chakra massages can release as much tension as a regular massage with more lasting benefits. Visualizing color and channeling energy are profound healing tools and can enhance not only your sex life but all areas of your life!

sexy
star signs

SEXY SPELLS

If you know what turns on a particular sign it can only
propel your lovemaking into a truly enchanting realm!

There are 12 star signs grouped into the four magickal
elements of Witchcraft – air, earth, fire and water.

Air signs are: Gemini, Libra and Aquarius

These are the thinkers of the zodiac. Air signs like people
to say what they mean and love stimulating conversation.
To seduce an air sign, don't come on too strong, they
may feel smothered. Let a Gemini know you like them
by showing interest in everything they do and having
interesting things to say yourself. A hint of naughtiness
turns them on! Librans love beauty and are turned on
by style and good taste. Mr Libra loves a lady who makes
the effort to look good. Aquarians can be cold. Respect

their independence and show that you share their ideas,
but don't push sex on them. Let them
make the first move. Generally, dirty talk is great for
air signs, but don't get too crude too quickly.
A mutual masturbation session can appeal to
their sexual senses too!

Earth signs are: Taurus, Virgo and Capricorn

These signs are very grounded and can be sceptical
of anything too gushy and overly romantic. They are
the boss and like to know where they stand. Taurus is
very sensual and loves good food and wine and presents.
Virgos love order and tidiness and can be very skilful
between the sheets – they also like good food, wine
and clothing. Turn on Mr Virgo by flashing the top
of a stocking. Capricorns are turned on by successful

people – they can be very lusty and are comfortable in their bodies. Capricorns are often the best for a one-night stand as they can separate sex from emotional commitment. Earth signs love threesomes, oral sex and using food as a seductive tool (try smearing chocolate all over them and licking it off). This can drive them wild!

Fire signs are: Aries, Leo and Sagittarius

The fire signs are very passionate and expressive. They get turned on by larger-than-life fantasy and lots of excitement – romance and drama appeals to their senses. Aries love a challenge and can be quite demanding once they decide they're interested. Make a fuss of Ms Aries and Mr Aries but maintain

an occasional aloofness to both and they will be wrapped
around your finger. Leos need to be the centre of
attention – but initially playing hard to get will work
wonders for attracting Mr Leo and Ms Leo. Sagittarians
can be incurable bed-hoppers, but as long as you keep
it interesting they should stay around – try doing it in
unusual places, like a phone booth! Fire signs like sex
with clothes on as well as dress ups and sex toys.
Watching porno can do it for them too.

Water signs are: Cancer, Scorpio and Pisces

It's all about feelings when it comes to water signs and
they are sensitive and sensual. Caring, closeness,
atmosphere and understanding will get you in.
Cancer loves to feel like you care only for them. Let
Cancerians know you're hot for them, as sometimes their

sensitivity will blind them to your interest. They are
generally highly sexed, seduce them in the moonlight
for a wild time. Scorpios are the sex maniacs of the
zodiac, but they respect warmth and genuine feelings
too. Pisces love feeling looked after. Piscean men can be
very sensual and love pleasing their women and Piscean
women are eternal romantics. Tell them you need
them and they will be there. Water signs also love oral
sex, sensual massage and sex in the shower.

THE PLEASURE PRESENT

Expert lovemaking can become a full-time occupation. Sex, of course, is the basic drive that fuels just about all of human experience and activities. However when you think of all the potential seduction scenes there are to set, the different toys there are to play with and the different sexual techniques from Kama Sutra to tantra to master – well you see what I mean! But putting aside all the clever techniques and props there is one sure-fire skill that never fails to please – it's what I call "The Pleasure Present".

The ability to be completely in the moment when lovemaking cannot be underestimated. Wonderful lovers take the time to really feel and focus on their partners – and the best way to enhance this ability is to take the time to really feel and focus on yourself.

The Ultimate Sexy Self Ritual

This ritual is for girls and guys and is profoundly transforming and a little difficult – unless you are naturally narcissistic, which isn't a bad thing necessarily!

YOU WILL NEED:
A private space (bedroom or bathroom)
1 full-length mirror
4 red candles
A bowl of water with a clear quartz crystal resting in it
(to positively charge)
Vanilla, musk, patchouli or ylang-ylang incense –
burn them all or pick one or two scents
Natural massage oil that you have blended yourself from
1 cup of almond, sunflower or other base and to which you
have added sandalwood and ylang-ylang (7 drops each).
Alternatively, you could buy a ready-made
"sensual" massage oil blend
Sea salt

Set up your ritual space by sprinkling a circle of salt around the mirror, large enough for you to sit within. This helps purify and contain the energies within your sacred space. Light the red candles, 2 either side of the mirror and 2 at the outer edge of the circle, so that you can sit within their light. Place the incense in front of the mirror, but do not light yet.

Take a bath to which you have added some sandalwood, ylang-ylang or geranium essential oil (maybe the guys would like cedar or patchouli) and float away any stress or tension.

When you are ready sit naked within your sacred circle and light the incense. Dip your hands in the charged water and sprinkle some around you. Your circle is now blessed by the elemental energies of earth (salt), fire

(candles), air (incense), water — and ready for magick.
As the incense billows up in front of the mirror take a
deep breath and close your eyes. Focus on your solar
plexus (centered just under your ribcage) and take
another deep breath, this time see the air that is flowing
into you as a pure, clear orange and see it swirl around
your solar plexus before diffusing through your entire
body. This orange light is the color of joy and
fulfilment – qualities that you are exploring within yourself in order to offer to and share them with your lover.

When your body is glowing orange in your mind's eye,
see the flames of the four candles glow larger and their
light extend in beams to meet above your head in a
spiralling, woven canopy of heat and light. Sense that
you are in a cocoon of all that is sensual and pleasurable
and open your eyes to gaze at yourself in the mirror.

Dip your hands in the massage oil and slowly begin to
caress your body. See your skin glow shiny and silken in
the soft candlelight. Keep your eye contact with yourself
as you repeat this mantra, either aloud or silently:

*"In the center of love am I
my sex is holy my body divine"*

Say these words slowly and savor their profound
nature. Often self-pleasuring is portrayed as
dirty or kinky and the key to the success of this ritual
is to replace that with a sensuous appreciation of
the sacredness of sexuality.

When your skin is coated with oil begin to slowly
masturbate taking your time to explore yourself. Try
to focus your mind in the exact moment you are in –
don't start to imagine a raunchy sex scene that you may
have once enjoyed or think you would like to! Focus
instead entirely on the sensations in your body, the soft
candlelight, the heady scent of the incense – what you

are cultivating is the ability to be entirely focused on
and in the moment of pure pleasure – this is the skill
that will make you a truly exceptional lover.

Keep masturbating to orgasm and as you come let the
sensation flood through your whole body as if you are
suspended in an ocean of pure pleasure. If you have
really stayed in the pleasure present your orgasm will
be stronger and longer and felt in a more divine
context than perhaps you normally experience it.

As the orgasmic sensations ebb away sit still and again
focus on exactly what you are feeling. Stroke and
massage your body as an affirmation of its extraordinary
ability to be the centre of such pleasure.

Look into your eyes in the mirror and say
this affirmation:

"Pleasure is the principle Divine
in my hands uniquely mine.
Physical passion, spiritual bliss,
the gifts of the Goddess are mine to give."

When you are next with your lover take the time to
really feel and focus on the moment. Be aware of the
honor that is to share another's extraordinary body.
You are the centre of the Universe and so is your
partner. In this enhanced, appreciative state, making
love, whether to a new lover or to your intimate
partner of 30 years, is always profound, exciting,
uplifting and enormously satisfying.

THE GOOD, SEXY OIL

Here are some essential oil blends that you either mix
in a base oil (a dessertspoon of jojoba or sweet
almond oil) to make a seriously sexy scent to anoint
yourself with or burn in an oil burner to turn
your environment into a pleasure pen!

Sexy scent no. 1
2 drops petitgrain
2 drops clove
2 drops geranium

Sexy scent no. 2
2 drops geranium
2 drops clary sage
2 drops patchouli

Super-sexy for girls, especially if you're feeling a bit
pre- or post-menstrual or menopausal – the above
scents will sex you up!

Sexy scent no. 3
2 drops mandarin
2 drops clove
2 drops patchouli

Sexy scent no. 4
2 drops orange
2 drops cedar
2 drops patchouli

Super-sexy for boys, especially if you're feeling the pressure to perform and are afraid you won't rise to the occasion – the above scents will lift you (or it) up!

Sexy scent no. 5
2 drops ylang-ylang
2 drops neroli
2 drops sandalwood
2 drops cinnamon
2 drops ginger

This scent packs a super-unisexy punch! Douse yourselves in it and be prepared to be transported!

SEXY COLOR BREATHING

Color can positively affect physical and emotional
health; two important things for magickal sex! Color
comes from light, which is a form of energy, and each
color has its own frequency, wavelength and effect on the
physical and emotional body.

The seven colors of the rainbow are red, orange,
yellow, green, blue, indigo and violet. Two of these,
red and orange, are great for enhancing sexual
confidence and pleasure. Add pink to these and you
have a sexy palette with which to play to get the
most out of your sensuality.

How to Sexy Color Breathe

Sit upright in a quiet, dark space. With your back against
a wall and your legs crossed or straight in front of you is
good. Close your eyes and take a deep breath.

With your next breath see the air slowly start to glow
with your chosen color. With each breath the color
increases until the air is vivid and intense. See this color
swirling in and out of your lungs. When this
is clear with your next breath, see the color start
to move from the base of your lungs towards your
uterus, ovaries and vagina (a beautiful inverted
triangle) for the girls and for the boys an upright
triangle centered over the testicles and penis. With
each breath now see your triangle of light glow brighter
and brighter. Sense a light and euphoric feeling emanate
throughout your entire body from these sacred triangles.

When the feeling is very strong, let the color burst from your triangle through your whole body so that it glows potent and full of color. Stay with this feeling and vision for a few more breaths, then slowly open your eyes, maintain the feeling for a few more breaths and then relax. You will notice increasingly positive effects from color breathing the more you do it.

THE SEXY COLORS

Orange

For genuine joy, confidence and stamina. Orange can help with menstrual problems, menopausal problems and prostate problems.

Red

For passion, energy and creativity. Red can also help with fertility problems and fatigue (do some red color breathing after a long day at work when your partner is randy and you feel like going to sleep, you'll rev up!).

Pink

For sensuality, arousal and confidence in your body, pink can also be good if you are recovering from an unhappy relationship, it helps you break with the past and embrace new situations.

ON A SEXY HIGH

Have sex after you've been to the gym or had a good workout running – whilst you are on a post-exercise endorphin high you will have more energy and stamina for longer sexual pleasure.

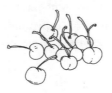

SEXY SUBSTANCES

Here is a selection of sexy substances that are fairly easily obtainable from a well-stocked health food store.

Some are used in the Sexy Spells and others are for
your pure experimentation and delight!

Cubeb Berries

These spicy little Asian berries are a renowned
aphrodisiac for men. Grind a small handful into
powder and mix with half a cup of runny honey to form
a paste. Take a teaspoon daily to prolong erections.

Damiana

Damiana is a Mexican shrub. Prepared as a tea or
smoked, macerated in alcohol or burnt as incense,
it acts as a powerful aphrodisiac for women and men
as well as a tonic for the sexual organs. If stored with
quartz crystal it is said to increase in potency.

Horny Goat Weed

Is there really such a thing? Absolutely! It is an ancient Chinese herb (yin yang huo) that is gaining increasing popularity in the West for its ability as a male aphrodisiac, menstrual regulator and relaxant. You can buy capsules of the herb or prepare a tincture by putting a handful of dried horny goat weed in a sterilized (boiled) glass bowl, covering with good-quality vodka or brandy (vodka tastes slightly better for this), covering with cloth and sealing with a rubber band. Leave it somewhere warm and dark (maybe in a cupboard next to a stove) for two weeks and then strain and keep in a dark glass bottle. Take a teaspoon in a small glass of room temperature water three times a day, preferably not with food.

Kava

I had a wonderful experience drinking kava in the South Pacific islands of Vanuatu. As long as it's not prepared too strongly it can be a subtle aphrodisiac that suffuses your body with a sense of contentment and well-being. I drank it the traditional way out of half a coconut after the roots had been prepared by a lovely ni-Vanuatu man

– that is, he chewed them voraciously until they were soggy with his spit, spat them in a bucket, poured in some water and scooped out a shell for me! Lots of fun! I was feeling very mellow until about my sixth half-shell, after which I started to feel quite ill!

The ni-Vanuatu women generally don't drink kava but they say it's great for keeping their notoriously volatile men calm and pleasing in the bedroom!

Prepare your own kava by taking 30 grams (one ounce) of the powder and simmering in two cups of coconut milk or just water if you prefer – don't boil, just let it infuse for 10 minutes, pour into cups, perhaps stir in some honey, and then let the kava powder settle before sipping slowly.

Mandrake

The root of this herb grows in the shape of a person and is much prized as a sexual potency totem. They are very rare and probably it would be best to grow one yourself from the seed. This takes about nine months after which you can carefully excavate the root (be sure to leave a drop of your own blood in the dent of soil from where the root is pulled as an offering and to forge a bond with mandrake's magickal powers). Wash and dry the root carefully and hang it upside down in a dark place to dry. When it is dry suspend it over your bed by red cord or wrap it in red cloth and keep it on a mantel or shelf in your bedroom. It can also encourage fertility, so keep it around if you are trying for a baby.

Saw Palmetto

The berries of this small palm tree have been proven to help with prostate problems and when prepared with damiana can be a good hormone balancing tonic for men and women. Take half a handful of the berries and one handful of damiana leaf, simmer in three cups of water for 10 minutes, strain, sweeten with honey and drink twice a day at least 20 minutes before food.

Schizandra

A Chinese berry beginning to be popularized in the West as a potent aphrodisiac (take it in capsules). It can help the body adapt to stress so can be helpful for men and women who find it hard to relax at the end of the day and take time out for themselves and some loving!

Spices

Cinnamon, cardamom, cumin, ginger, galangal – all these wonderful Indian/Asian spices are said to guarantee happy sexual activity to late in life. They

stimulate peripheral circulation and magickally are
considered to bestow maximum pleasure and
contentment in all physical expressions of love.

Yohimbe

The bark of this West African tree is a true and potent
aphrodisiac that science acknowledges above all other
herbal aphrodisiacal claims. However, it has a drastic
effect on the circulation by increasing and then
constricting blood flow, which can be great for sensual
sensitivity of the sex organs but dangerous for anyone
with diabetes or blood pressure problems. You can try
a weak brew – half a teaspoon of the dried bark to 2 cups
of water, simmered for 10 minutes, strained and drunk
with a little honey. Don't have alcohol with it and if
you want to try anything stronger, speak to a qualified
herbalist and your doctor.

EVERY DAY'S A SEXY DAY!

We get so caught up in our everyday, stressful lives that taking the time to spoil ourselves, to do even little things that pleasure us, becomes a poor second or third to doing the housework, feeding the kids, studying for exams or blotting ourselves out with alcohol or food. Magick is the art of transformation with will and one of the best ways to kick-start this process is by transforming your physical environment.

So surround yourself with things that pleasure you, erotic objects, sweet and pungent scents and lush flowers. Splurge and buy beautiful bedlinen and a throw rug in soft velour or fur to make your bed a haven of pleasure. Burn aromatherapy oils, use candles in the

evening instead of electricity, and play soft sensual music
instead of turning the TV or the radio on as
soon as you get home from work.

Shower the stress of the day away, spray on your
favourite perfume or aftershave and, rather than throw
on some old sweats, ceremoniously clothe yourself in
a heavy cotton bathrobe to relax in or a silky wrap
to swish against your skin.

Go without wearing underwear for the sensuous feeling
this evokes. Or alternatively splurge and buy the best and
wear it, not on a special occasion but every day.

These seemingly simple actions will have a far-reaching
effect – primarily because they will affirm to you your
self-respect and self-love. Your dream magickal love
life starts with you.

YOU SEXY FEAST

There are many foods perfect for a seductive feast.
Here's a menu guaranteed to tease and please!

Set the scene with lots of scented candles and vases
of fresh flowers. The TV and the radio must be off, the
phone taken off the hook and cell phones
banished. Wear something seductive or why not nothing
at all. Except perhaps an apron and high heels!
Maybe the boys can just wear the apron!
A sense of humor is very sexy too.

For starters, serve some of the best champagne you can
afford. Veuve Cliquot is my favorite, but if that is
breaking the budget, buy a cheaper alternative. Finely
chop some strawberries and float them on the surface.

For the ultimate seductive, I think, stick to
champagne, the bubbles will keep you both feverish
with anticipation, or maybe white wine – if you hit the
red you may get sleepy and heavy and that's the
opposite effect we want here!

In fact the following love food suggestions are
intentionally light and easily digestible so that you will
have plenty of energy for what comes later.

APPETIZER

Amorous Artichokes

Remove the stem of the artichokes, cut one inch from
the top and discard. Stand them in boiling water to cover.
Cook over a medium heat until the bottoms are easily
pierced (anywhere from 30 to 45 minutes). Lift them
out carefully and place on a rack to drain.

Whilst the artichokes are cooking prepare this divine
spiced butter. Remove seeds and braise half a sweet red
bell pepper and one jalapeno chilli. Peel off the skin and
macerate the flesh. Crush one clove of garlic and cook in
a little butter, add the pepper flesh and 50 grams butter.
Melt over a very low heat and add a little pepper
and salt to taste.

To serve remove the leaves of the artichoke, dip them
in the butter and hand-feed them to your lover so that
he/she can suck the artichoke flesh and butter off
your fingertips.

MAIN COURSE

A salad of fresh vegetables including avocado, arugula
(rocket lettuce), endive, tomatoes, fennel and mush-
rooms will invigorate and charge up the sex hormones
(even include celery for an extra boost). A dressing of
¼ cup of virgin olive oil, 1 tablespoon balsamic vinegar
and a handful of finely chopped fresh basil will ensure
harmony and good digestion (important if you want
to romp in the sack straight after dinner!).

Oysters with a squeeze of fresh lime or lemon juice
blended with a little tamari (soy sauce) and chopped
chilli are great to put a sparkle in the blood! Other
shellfish like lobster, mussels and clams are proven
aphrodisiacs – the Spanish seafood dish, paella, would
be perfect for seafood lovers.

Seafood Paella
(SERVES 2)

100g/ (¼ lb) shrimp, peeled (reserve the shells)
Pinch of saffron threads
Salt to taste
2 tablespoons extra-virgin olive oil
100g/ (¼ lb) scallops (or calamari, cut into rings)
½ small onion, coarsely grated
3 garlic cloves, peeled and crushed (minced)
1 small ripe tomato, peeled then coarsely grated

150g/ ¾ cup medium-grain rice
4 small mussels or clams, scrubbed
½ lemon, cut into wedges for garnish

Boil 560ml/two cups of salted water in a small saucepan. Add the shrimp shells and simmer, covered, for about 10 minutes. Strain the stock, discard the shells and return the stock to the saucepan. Heat the saffron very gently under a grill (broiler), crush the threads with the back of a spoon and add to the stock. Add more salt to taste, if necessary. Set aside.

In a 14-inch paella pan (or frying pan or skillet), heat the oil on high. Dry the shrimp and scallops (or calamari) with kitchen paper. When the oil is hot, sauté the shrimp and scallops until almost cooked through, about 2 minutes. Transfer to a plate and set aside. Reduce the heat to medium and sauté the onion and garlic until the onion softens, about 5 minutes. Add the tomato, season with salt and sauté the mixture for 10–15 minutes until it has darkened and is a thick purée. Meanwhile, bring the stock back to a simmer.

When the tomato mixture is ready, add the rice to the
pan. Sauté the mixture until the rice is no longer
opaque, about 1 minute. Increase the heat to
medium-high. Reserve about 60ml/ ¼ cup of the stock
and pour the rest into the rice mixture. Stir or shake
the pan to evenly distribute the rice. As the liquid begins
to boil, arrange the mussels or clams in the pan,
pushing them below the level of the liquid.
From this point on, do not stir the rice.

Cook the paella on medium-high, rotating the pan to
distribute the heat. When the rice has absorbed much
of the liquid, after about 8 minutes, reduce the heat.
Continue to simmer, rotating the pan as necessary, until
all the liquid has been absorbed, about 10 minutes.
Test the rice – if it is not done but all the liquid has
been absorbed, add the reserved stock and cook a few
minutes more. Arrange the shrimp and scallops
(or calamari) in the pan.

Cover the pan with foil and cook gently for another
2 minutes. Increase the heat and cook until the bottom

layer of rice starts to caramelize, about 2 minutes.
The rice may crackle somewhat, but do not allow it to
burn. Remove the paella from the heat and allow it to
stand for 5 minutes, still covered, before serving.
Paella is best eaten straight from the pan
(don't forget to squeeze over some lemon juice).

Alternatively, a simple, lush medium-rare steak, smeared
with seeded mustard (to enliven and invigorate), or a
sleek, poached chicken breast in a sauce of garlic and
tarragon (aligned with the Feminine essence of the
Universe), will inspire delight and desire.

Garlic and Tarragon Sauce

YOU WILL NEED:
4 teaspoons of unsalted butter
3 cloves of garlic
2 tablespoons buckwheat or unbleached flour
1 cup of vegetable stock
1 cup of soy or dairy milk
2 teaspoons of tarragon
1 teaspoon of cracked black pepper

Melt the butter in a medium saucepan over a low heat, add the garlic crushed and sauté until brown. Slowly stir in the flour – it will go quite cakey – stir constantly, turn up the heat a tiny bit and cook for two minutes. Slowly stir in the stock, tarragon, pepper and bring to the boil. Simmer for five minutes stirring constantly. Then turn the heat right down, stir in the milk and heat – but don't let it boil! Pour generously over the chicken – yum!

For vegetarians the above sauce is also divine served over a sweet potato and lentil terrine (the phallic shape of this root is appropriate for this dinner!). Vegans can replace the butter with soy or tofu "spread" and use soya milk –

and actually this dish is one of my absolute faves from my
vegan days and has been successfully used
in a few seduction scenes!

Sweet Potato and Lentil Terrine

YOU WILL NEED:
*4 medium orange sweet potatoes, peeled and
thinly sliced
1 can of precooked lentils
1 medium brown onion
3 cloves of garlic, crushed
Butter
2 ripe red tomatoes
Cracked black pepper
½ cup virgin olive oil
Wholemeal breadcrumbs for topping*

Preheat the oven to 180°C (350°F). In a pan sauté
the garlic in a little butter and then add the finely
chopped onion and sauté, finally add the finely diced
tomatoes and then the lentils. Stir through.

Toss the sweet potato and black pepper in olive oil and then layer with the lentil mixture in a greased, shallow baking dish (Pyrex is good). Bake for at least 45 minutes but up to an hour.

Mix the crumbs through with either a little melted butter or olive oil with your fingertips until blended. Remove the terrine from the oven, spread the crumbs over the top and bake for another 10 minutes until brown.

Drizzle with the garlic and tarragon sauce – mmm my stomach is rumbling as I write this!

DESSERT

You of course! Or maybe you would like to tantalize your lover with these chocolate-dipped strawberries. Why not place one in your mouth and let him/her gently bite into it with you.

YOU WILL NEED:
*200g (½lb) of sweet or bittersweet chocolate
(or a cup of choc chips)
A couple of shots of Irish cream liqueur
Large sweet strawberries*

Break the chocolate into small pieces and melt
in a bowl in the microwave for about 30 seconds.
Stir in the liqueur and then dip the tips of the
strawberries in the mixture. Place them on a rack
and put in the fridge to set.

Simpler as far as preparation goes but a just-as-sexy
dessert is a succulent red ice lolly (popsical)! Gaze
into your lover's eyes and suggestively suck it and maybe
even trail it over their skin and other appropriate
regions and lick off the sweet liquid!

Finally, your sexy feast will be a sure success if you
approach it with a true and deep desire to make
your partner feel like a God or Goddess. Focus on
them and their desirous needs and yours will more
than be met too!

AN INCREDIBLY IMPORTANT MAGICKAL TIP

Magick works with the intent you fuel it. There are four simple ways to ensure that your personal sex magick is truly enchanting.

1. Before embarking on any magickal task take a deep breath and center yourself (i.e., let go of any tension or concerns – you can worry about day-to-day stresses later).
2. Focus on the present moment only.
3. Have unshakeable belief in your own infinite capabilities.
4. Smile!

SUPPLIES

There is an extensive list of international suppliers at my website **www.fionahorne.com**. Otherwise, everything I have suggested in this book should be available at a well-stocked health food store and/or New Age/ alternative-living gift store. You may also use the useful contacts at the back of this book.

USEFUL CONTACTS FOR ALL YOUR MAGICKAL SUPPLIES

AUSTRALIA

Victoria

The Esoteric Bookshop
Glen Arcade
675 Glenferrie Rd
Hawthorn 3122
Ph: 03 9818 1988
www.esotericbookshop.com.au

Spellbox
Shop 17 Royal Arcade
Bourke St
Melbourne 3000
Ph: 03 9639 7077

Queensland

Circle Bookshop
Floor 1, 132 Albert St
Brisbane 4000
Ph: 07 3229 3208

Bent Books
205a Boundary St
West End 4101
Ph: 07 3846 5004
hello@bentbooks.com.au

Underworld Realm
1st Floor, 144 Adelaide St
Brisbane 4000
Ph: 07 3236 1063

Celtic Karma
66 Boundary St
West End 4810
Ph: 07 3846 5581

Wizard's Realm
Shop 25 The Mark Centre
Orchid Ave
Surfers Paradise 4217
**wizardsrealm@wizardsrealm.
com.au**

The Witches Cauldron
Shop 9, 79 Grafton St
Cairns 4870
Ph: 07 4051 2100

ACT

Inner Harmony Australia
Shop 3F14, Level 3
Canberra Centre
Civic
Ph: 02 6247 1987

New South Wales

Adyar Bookshop
230 Clarence St
Sydney 2000
Ph: 02 9267 8509
www.adyar.com.au

Mysterys
First Floor
314–322 Darling St
Balmain 2041
Ph: 02 9818 2274

Abracadabra Australia
89 Cronulla St
Cronulla 2230
Ph: 02 9544 5600

Inner Realms
Shop 3, 324 Sandgate Rd
Shortland 2307
Ph: 02 4955 0080

South Australia

Marbri Witchcraft Shop
1/581 North East Rd
Gilles Plain 5086
Ph: 0401 360 494

Cosmic Pages Metaphysical
Booksellers
338–340 King William St
Adelaide 5000
Ph: 08 8231 9105 or
08 8231 6720
Fax: 08 8231 0659

Quantum Bookshop
113 Melbourne St
North Adelaide 5006
Ph: 08 8267 1579
Fax: 08 8239 2288

The Eternal Spirit
67–69 Goodwood Rd
Wayville 5034
Ph: 08 8271 9666
Fax: 08 8271 9715

Western Australia

The Alchemist
6 Market St
Fremantle 6160
Ph: 08 9430 6779

Down To Earth Bookshop
790 Hay St
Perth 6000
Ph: 08 9321 9752

Book & Crystal Den
87A Hannan St
Kalgoorlie 6430
Ph: 08 9091 3288

Kimberley Bookshop
4 Napier Tce
Broome 6725
Ph: 08 9192 1844

Tasmania

Berkana Bookshop
118 St John St
Launceston 7250
Ph: 03 6334 3068

The Akashic Bookshop
Shop 7/60 Elizabeth Mall
Hobart 7000
Ph: 03 6231 9107
*(Upper Level Cat and
Fiddle Arcade)*

United Kingdom

Seven Stars
4 New St
Dudley, West Mids
DY1 1LP
Ph: 01384 233630

The Wyrd Shop
154 Canongate
Edinburgh
EH8 8DD
Ph: 0131 577 2293

Arcania
17 Union Passage
Bath BA1

Zen
Brindley Place
Broad St
Birmingham

Winfalacons
28 Ship St
Brighton

Mind Matters
21 The Borough
Canterbury CT1

Green Man Bookshop and
Gallery
24 South St, Eastbourne
East Sussex BN21 4XB
Ph: 01323 735364

Opal Moon
Decourcys Arcade
Cresswell Lane
Glasgow G12 3AA
Ph: 0141 338 6010

Pilgrams
1a College Court
Westgate St
Gloucester GL1

Spooks
22 Main St
Haworth

Spirit of the Ages
28–29 Byram Arcade
Westgate, Huddersfield

Page One Bookshop
9 Princes Avenue
Hull HU5

Sacred Earth
6 Upper Orwell St
Ipswich IP1

Gaia
7 Regent Place
Leamington Spa

Atlantis Bookshop
49a Museum St
Bloomsbury,
London WC1A 1LY
Ph: 020 7405 2120
Fax: 020 7430 0535

Spiveys Web
90 Chestergate
Macclesfield SK11

New Aeon Books
11–112 Tib St
Manchester M4

Magenta
12 Peddar St
Morecomb LA4

Enchanted
95 Caversham Rd
Reading RD1

Sacred Moon
27 Wyle Cop
Shrewsbury SY1

Four Elements
17a Lower Hillgate
Stockport SK1

Dragons Breath
Hollybush Studio
Fore St
Tintagel

Joy
13 Hopmarket Yard
Worcester WR5

Odyssey
66 Walmgate
York YO1

America

Morgana's Chamber
242 W10th St
New York
Ph: 212 243 3415

Triple Moon Inc
15 Power House Circle
Needham Ma. 02492
Ph: 781 453 0363
www.triplemoon.com

The Mythic Images Collection
10266 Old Redwood Highway
Penngrove CA 94951
Ph: 707 795 8047
Fax: 707 792 0143
www.MythicImages.com

Ancient Ways
4075 Telegraph Avenue
Oakland CA 94609
Ph: 510 653 3244
Fax: 510 653 3269
www.ancientways.com

Points of Light
4358 Stearns St
Long Beach CA 90815
Ph: 562 985 3388
Fax: 562 986 7400
www.pointsoflight.com

Isis Books and Gifts
5701 E. Colfax Ave
Denver CO 80220
Ph: 303 321 0867
www.isisbooks.com

Ravens Flight
5042 Vineland Avenue
North Hollywood CA 91601
Ph: 1 88 84 RAVEN
www.cyberWitch.com/raven

Panpipes Magickal
Marketplace
1641 Cahuenga Boulevard
Hollywood CA
Ph: 323 462 7078
www.panpipes.com

Psychic Eye Bookshop
13435 Ventura Boulevard
Sherman Oaks CA 91423
Ph: 818 906 8263
www.pebooks.com
*Check their website for a full
listing of all their stores*

Thorsons

Directions for Life

This online sanctuary is packed with information, inspiration and guidance to help you on the path to physical and spiritual well-being. Drawing on the integrity and vision of our authors and titles, and with health advice, articles, astrology, tarot, a meditation zone, author interviews and events listings, Thorsons.com is a great alternative to help create space and peace in our lives.

So if you've always wondered about practicing yoga, following an allergy-free diet, using the tarot or getting a life coach, we can point you in the right direction.

Make www.thorsons.com your online sanctuary.

www.thorsons.com